IN THEIR OWN WORDS

LEWIS AND CLARK

George Sullivan

SCHOLASTIC
REFERENCE

ACKNOWLEDGMENTS
Many people helped me by providing helpful background information and illustrations to
be used in this book. I'm very grateful to them all. Special thanks are due: Ellen Thomasson,
Missouri Historical Society; Maja Keech, Division of Prints and Photographs, Library of
Congress; Sammye Meadows, Lewis and Clark Trail Heritage Foundation; James T. Parker,
Archival Research International; Scott DeHaven, American Philosophical Society; Ellen
Cordes, Beinecke Rare Book and Manuscript Library, Yale University; Heather Egan,
National Portrait Gallery; Diane Keller, Montana Historical Society; Ron Williams, Lewis
and Clark State Park, Onawa, Iowa; Courtney DeAngelis, Amon Carter Museum; Mikki
Tint, Oregon Historical Society; Grace E. Linden, Sioux City Public Museum; Susan
Albrecht, Montana Department of Commerce; Wallace Keck and B. H. Rucker, Missouri
Department of Natural Resources; Steve Matz, Salmon & Challis National Forests; Betsy
Gabelsberger, Missouri Division of Tourism; Mary Ethel Emanuel, Nebraska Division of
Travel and Tourism; and Don Wigal.

GEORGE SULLIVAN
NEW YORK CITY

Library of Congress Cataloguing-in-Publication Data
Sullivan, George, 1927—
Lewis and Clark / by George Sullivan
p. cm.—(In their own words)
Includes bibliographical references (p.) and index.
Summary: Recounts the story of the Lewis and Clark Expedition to explore the uncharted
western wilderness, placing it in its historical context.
1. Lewis and Clark Expedition (1804—1806) Juvenile literature. 2. West (U.S.)—
Discovery and exploration Juvenile literature. 3. Lewis, Meriwether, 1774—1809
Juvenile literature. 4. Clark, William, 1770—1838 Juvenile literature. [1. Lewis and
Clark Expedition (1804—1806) 2. West (U.S.)—Discovery and exploration.] I. Title.
II. Series: In their own words (Scholastic)
F592.7.S85 1999   978'.02—dc21   99-27629   CIP
ISBN 0-439-09553-0
10 9 8 7 6 5 4 3   0/0 01 02 03
Composition by Brad Walrod
Printed in the U.S.A.   40
First printing, November 1999

CONTENTS

INTRODUCTION

"**H**AVING FOR MANY DAYS PAST confined myself to the boat, I determined to devote this day to amuse myself on shore with my gun and view the interior of the country lying between the river and Corvus Creek. Before sunrise I set out with six of my best hunters."

These words are from the pen—the quill pen—of Meriwether Lewis. Along with William Clark, Lewis led the famous voyage of discovery into what is now the northwestern United States. It was a vast wilderness area at the time.

During their long journey, both Lewis and William Clark kept a detailed daily record of what they saw. What's written above is from

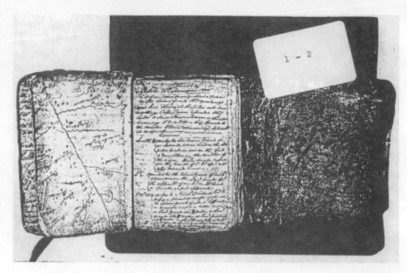

One of William Clark's elk-skin-bound field journals

Lewis's journal entry for Monday, September 17, 1804. The explorers were traveling north on the Missouri River. They were passing through what is now South Dakota.

In the entry, Lewis told of seeing hawks, small wolves, and some polecats. He saw herds of buffalo. He also saw several herds of antelope. He described the antelope as being "shye and watchfull [shy and watchful]." (Neither Lewis nor Clark could have won a spelling contest. Misspelled words are common in their journals.)

Lewis spoke of the plants and trees he sighted. He

noticed a grove of plum trees. The fruit was much the same as back home in Virginia. He remarked how green the grass was.

Reading what Lewis and Clark wrote, one gets the feeling of almost being with the explorers. Each man made notes during the day. When time allowed, they wrote in their journals.

Writing was never an easy task for the explorers. They had to carefully mix water and powdered ink to get an ink supply. They used a quill to write. A quill is the tip of a feather, often from a goose. It had to be dipped into ink after every second or third word. If Lewis and Clark wrote at night, they worked by lantern light.

The two men wrote in small notebooks. As each notebook was filled, it was put into a small tin box. The box was sealed to make it waterproof.

A good number of the Lewis and Clark journals have survived to this day. Eighteen are in the collection of the American Philosophical Society of Philadelphia. The Missouri Historical Society in St. Louis also has some of the journals.

The Lewis and Clark Expedition is one of the

great adventure stories in American history. The explorers' journals that report on that trip are, in the words of historian Stephen Ambrose, "a national literary treasure."

The journals help to answer questions about the journey. They are a primary source. Primary sources are actual records that have been handed down from the past. Diaries, speeches, and letters are primary sources.

Along with the journals of Lewis and Clark, Lincoln's Gettysburg Address is a primary source. So are census records. A photograph of your grandmother is a primary source.

A secondary source is a description of an event written by someone who did not witness it. Textbooks are secondary sources. *The World Book Encyclopedia* and other encyclopedias are secondary sources.

Serious students use primary sources in writing reports or biographies. Primary sources such as the journals of Lewis and Clark have enormous value. They give us the actual words of those involved in the event.

They're also a treat to read. Says Stephen Ambrose: "Reading the [Lewis and Clark] journals puts you in a canoe with them. You see the country through their eyes. You and the captains are in a constant state of surprise, because as you read, and as they write, you never know what's around the bend of the river, or what will happen next."

"VOYAGE OF DISCOVERY"

JULY 4, 1803, WAS A GREAT DAY FOR Meriwether Lewis. The tall, slim, twenty-eight-year-old captain in the U.S. Army was ready for an awesome journey.

Just months before, President Thomas Jefferson named Lewis to head what he called a "Voyage of Discovery." Its goal was clear. Lewis was to explore the vast wilderness that is now the northwestern United States. These were lands unknown to Americans. On maps of the day, the region was a great blank space.

President Jefferson instructed Lewis to follow the Missouri River to its source. He hoped that

Lewis would find that the Missouri was linked to the Columbia River in the northwest.

That link would make for a direct route to the Pacific Ocean. This route was called the Northwest Passage. In a sense, it would open a highway across America.

At the time, all heavy loads moved by water. They floated downstream on rafts or large flat-bottomed craft called barges. They were towed upstream on barges. Mules, horses, or oxen drew the barges.

Of course, heavy cargo could also be moved by wagon. But there was a limit on how heavy a load an animal could pull on land.

Besides, the nation had few roads at the time. West of the Mississippi, there were scarcely any roads at all. There were only trails.

President Jefferson not only wanted Lewis to find a Northwest Passage. He was also hungry for information about the Native Americans who lived in the West. He wanted Lewis to learn all that he could about their customs and culture.

The president was curious about the land, too. Observe, he instructed, "the face of the country, its growth and vegetable productions . . . the animals of the country generally, and especially those not known in the U.S."

July 4, 1803, was also important because of a newspaper story. In Washington, the *National Intelligencer* reported that Emperor Napoleon Bonaparte of France had sold Louisiana to the United States.

The Louisiana Purchase is one of the most important events in American history. With it, the United States gained most of the land between the Mississippi River and the Rocky Mountains.

The U.S. Senate approved the purchase on October 20, 1803. The price agreed upon was $15 million. That amounts to about four cents an acre.

The Louisiana Purchase changed the expedition —or journey—that Lewis was to lead. It meant that he would be traveling in American territory as far as the Rocky Mountains. The Native Americans in the area were now living on United States soil. No

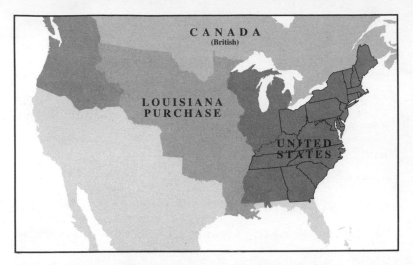

With the Louisiana Purchase, the United States doubled in size, gaining most of the land between the Mississippi River and the Rocky Mountains.

longer did the French rule them. Lewis would be telling the Native Americans that their "Great Father"—the president of the United States— lived in Washington.

There was also a political meaning to the Louisiana Purchase. Thomas Jefferson was a man of great vision. He saw the United States as a nation that one day would extend from the Atlantic Ocean to the Pacific. The Louisiana Purchase was a big leap forward in realizing that dream.

In Meriwether Lewis, Jefferson believed he had the perfect man to lead the expedition. Lewis's army experience had taught him to cope with life in the wilderness. While in the army, Lewis had been assigned to visit army posts in river cities along the Ohio River. He traveled on horseback. He had also traveled in small boats. He had become a skilled riverman as a result.

Lewis was stationed in Detroit early in 1801 when he received important news. Thomas Jefferson had been elected president. In Virginia, the Jeffersons had been neighbors and friends of the Lewis family.

Within a week after being elected, Jefferson asked Lewis to become his private secretary. Lewis wasted no time in accepting the offer.

Lewis served as Jefferson's private secretary from 1801 to 1803. He lived in the president's house, which later became known as the White House. Jefferson treated him as a member of the family. The subject of exploring the continent west of the Mississippi was often discussed.

Thomas Jefferson was president of the United States from 1801 to 1809. He arranged the Louisiana Purchase and sent Lewis and Clark on their journey of exploration.

In a message to Congress on January 18, 1803, Jefferson proposed a "Voyage of Discovery" across the continent. Congress approved Jefferson's request. The expedition would soon be a reality.

Jefferson told Congress that the expedition could

be carried out by "an intelligent officer with ten or twelve chosen men." Jefferson knew exactly who that intelligent officer should be.

Jefferson did not announce that the job was open. He interviewed no other candidates. He asked for no one's advice. Meriwether Lewis was Jefferson's one and only choice.

CHAPTER 3

THE CAPTAINS

LEWIS REALIZED ALMOST FROM THE beginning that he could not lead the expedition by himself. He needed someone to share the burdens. He needed someone he could trust. He needed a friend.

Lewis thought of William Clark. Clark had been his commanding officer in the army.

In the months that they were together, Lewis had grown to like Clark. He respected him.

Lewis knew the Clark family. The Clarks had once lived in Albemarle County, Virginia. Lewis had been born in Albemarle County. He grew up there.

On June 19, 1803, Lewis wrote to Clark. He

told him of the expedition. He invited him to take part in it.

He explained to Clark that President Jefferson had named him to lead the expedition. But he wanted Clark to share that leadership role with him. Lewis wanted Clark's rank to be equal to his own.

Clark was at his Kentucky farm when he received Lewis's letter. He answered it the next day.

The mails were slow in those days. Lewis did not receive Clark's reply until very late in July 1803.

The letter brought the news that Lewis had been hoping for. Clark accepted Lewis's invitation. "I will cheerfully join you," Clark said, "and partake of the dangers, difficulties, and fatigues..."

With that letter, it became the Lewis and Clark Expedition. The two names became forever linked. Today, as Stephen Ambrose has noted, most Americans think of them as Lewisandclark.

Meriwether Lewis was born near Charlottesville, Virginia, on August 18, 1774. He was named for his mother, Lucy Meriwether.

Meriwether was the oldest boy born to Lucy and

*A pen-and-ink sketch of Meriwether Lewis.
Lewis was twenty-eight years-old when he
was asked to lead the expedition.*

her husband, William Lewis. The Lewises had the
Jeffersons as their neighbors. Thomas Jefferson was
William Lewis's friend.

When Meriwether Lewis was three years old,
tragedy struck the family. His father died of
pneumonia. Not long after, his mother remarried.

The family moved to Georgia when Meriwether Lewis was eight or nine. There he learned to love the outdoors. As a young boy, he became an expert hunter.

When Lewis was about thirteen, he returned to Virginia so he could get an education. There were no public schools in Virginia at the time. Parents sent their sons to private tutors. Usually the tutors were preachers or parsons.

Private tutors schooled Lewis for several years. When he had completed his studies, he planned to go to college. But his stepfather died. Lewis felt that it was his duty to stay at home and serve as head of the family. He took over the management of the family's 2,000-acre plantation.

Meriwether Lewis was twenty years old when President George Washington sent out a call for troops. They were needed to put down an uprising of farmers in western Pennsylvania. The farmers refused to pay a whiskey tax. The revolt became known as the Whiskey Rebellion.

Lewis volunteered. Not long after his enlistment,

he wrote to his mother to say that he was "...quite delighted with a soldier's life."

In the fall of 1795, Lewis was transferred to a rifle company made up of sharpshooters. The captain of the unit was William Clark.

The red-haired Clark was four years older than Lewis. He had been born in Caroline County, Virginia. He was the ninth child of John and Anne Rogers Clark.

When William Clark was fourteen, his family moved to a Kentucky plantation. He became a militiaman and took part in several campaigns against the Native Americans on the western border.

Young William Clark impressed his commanding officers. A letter to his eldest brother from one of the officers declared: "Your brother William has gone out as a cadet with Gen. Scott. He is a youth of solid and promising parts and as brave as [Julius] Caesar."

In 1792, Clark joined the U.S. Army. He served as an officer under the command of General Anthony Wayne. Clark was with Wayne at the

Strong and good-natured, William Clark was four years older than Lewis.

Battle of Fallen Timbers in 1794. The Native Americans were defeated. But 107 men from the U.S. Army were killed or wounded. The next year, Meriwether Lewis joined Clark's rifle company.

Clark left the army in 1796. He returned to the family plantation in Kentucky. There, in 1803, Clark received Lewis's letter asking him to join Lewis as a leader of the expedition.

From the start, Lewis and Clark worked together as a team. There was no tension between them.

Physically, the two men were much the same. Each was about six feet tall. Each was trim, strong, and broad-shouldered. Each could ride and hunt.

Lewis was the quieter of the two men. He was

more serious. He was somewhat moody. There were days that he liked to be by himself.

Clark was more talkative and outgoing. He had a quick smile and an easygoing manner.

Clark was more of a frontiersman than Lewis. He was at home in the backwoods, where he had spent much of his life.

Clark was familiar with the habits of wild animals. He drew a little. He illustrated his journals with pictures of birds, fish, and animals. He also made the expedition's maps.

Lewis was the expedition's naturalist. He wrote long descriptions of the plants and animals they saw. He collected plant, animal, and mineral specimens to be sent back to President Jefferson.

When the expedition was underway, Clark would normally be found in the long boat in which the explorers traveled. He set the course. He supervised the men who did the rowing.

Lewis often walked the shoreline, keeping the boat in view. His dog and his rifle were his only companions.

Clark's illustrations give life to his journals. This is his drawing of a dark-furred marten, an animal he called "The Fisher."

The Lewis and Clark Expedition was to become a great success story. In large part, that was due to the combined qualities of the two leaders. It was also due to their ability to work together so well.

CHAPTER 4

IVORY COMBS AND CALICO SHIRTS

H OW DO YOU PACK FOR A TRIP THAT is going to take two and half years and cover seven or eight thousand miles?

Once you start there will be no place to buy supplies. You must pack every single thing you need. You're going to be like a ship on the ocean or a desert caravan.

How do you begin?

Meriwether Lewis began with good rifles. He knew that powerful and accurate rifles in the hands of skilled hunters would mean a constant food supply. And rifles were important for self-defense.

Lewis went to the U.S. Army's arsenal at

Harpers Ferry, Virginia. There he bought fifteen long-barreled rifles. They were the first rifles especially designed for the army. Such a rifle could bring down a deer at two hundred yards.

Lewis did much of his shopping in Philadelphia during the summer of 1803. He also did some studying there.

From scholars in Philadelphia, Lewis learned how to classify plants and animals. He also learned how to determine where he was in the world by observing the stars.

Lewis's shopping list included hundreds of pounds of flour, ground corn, and salt.

He also bought a "portable soup" made of dried vegetables and other ingredients. By adding water to the mixture and boiling it, the explorers would get a hot meal.

Lewis supervised as blankets, books, and clothing were packed in seven big bundles. He used oilskin bags to protect scientific instruments. Such waterproof bags were also used for the journals that he and Clark planned to keep.

Lewis purchased sheets of oilcloth. Each measured eight by twelve feet. These were to be used as tents.

Lewis also bought fourteen bales of gifts for the Native Americans. He knew that they wanted such items as glass beads, scissors, brass thimbles, sewing thread, knives, ivory combs, and calico shirts.

Lewis also took along medals and certificates for Native American leaders. The United States had begun giving "peace medals" to the Native Americans as early as 1789. On one side, the medals carried a picture of the president. On the other side,

The peace medals given out by Lewis and Clark featured President Jefferson's image.

they displayed a pair of clasped hands and the words PEACE AND FRIENDSHIP. A colorful ribbon was used in hanging the medal around one's neck.

By the Fourth of July, Lewis had finished his shopping and studying in Philadelphia. He set out across the Appalachian Mountains to Pittsburgh. There he was having a keelboat built.

The keelboat was a type of boat often used on western rivers. The one that Lewis ordered was fifty-five feet long and eight feet wide. Across the deck were sturdy benches.

Along each side of the boat were large wooden lockers. The lids of the lockers could be raised for protection if the boat came under attack.

Lewis had a small cannon installed at the boat's bow—or front. It was mounted on a swivel. That way the cannon could be swung in one direction or the other.

The keelboat was also fitted with a mast—or pole. It was thirty-two feet in height. The mast could be raised or lowered. When the wind was favorable, the crew raised the mast and hoisted a large square sail.

Besides being rowed and sailed, the keelboat could also be poled. In poling, crew members stood and thrust long poles into the river bottom from the boat's bow. They pushed hard on the poles as they walked toward the boat's stern. The boat usually moved faster when it was being poled than rowed.

The expedition later added two smaller boats. These were sturdy, round-bottomed canoes. They were known as pirogues.

By the end of August, work had been completed on the keelboat. Lewis started down the Ohio River in it. He picked up Clark in Clarksville, Indiana. He also brought on board some of the first men who would be part of the expedition.

The trip down the Ohio River was not easy. The water level was very low that summer. The men frequently had to pull and push the boat across ridges of sand. In some spots, they had to hire teams of horses or oxen to do the pulling.

When they reached the Mississippi River, they turned upstream. They kept paddling until they reached the Wood River, just north of St. Louis.

The "Friends of Discovery" at the Lewis and Clark State Park in Onawa, Iowa, constructed this replica of the explorers' keelboat. The boat is used in retracing their travels on the Missouri River.

There they set up winter quarters. The site is sometimes called Camp DuBois. It is also called Camp Wood. Not far from their campsite, the captains could see the wide mouth of the Missouri River.

Several weeks before the expedition set out, Lewis received disturbing news. Lewis had promised Clark that he would be made a captain. He and Lewis would then be of equal rank. But the request was not granted. Instead, the War Department made it clear that Clark would be a lieutenant. That was below Lewis's rank.

Lewis was in St. Louis at the time. He wasted no time in writing to Clark at the Wood River camp. He told him the bad news. He added, "I think it will be best to let none of our party or any other persons know any thing about the grade [rank]..."

So it was that the two men simply ignored what the War Department had done, or had failed to do. During the long months of the expedition, the men never knew that Lewis actually outranked Clark. Both men were addressed as captains. Both men shared the leadership role through good times and bad.

UP THE WIDE MISSOURI

MAY 14, 1804, WAS A BANNER DAY for the explorers. It was the day that they were to leave the Wood River camp and begin their journey.

With the men pulling hard on the oars, the big keelboat and two pirogues moved out into the wide and muddy Missouri. A small group of well-wishers along the riverbank cheered.

Clark's journal for that day reads:

I Set out at 4 oClock P.M. in the presence of many of the neighboring inhabitents [inhabitants], and proceeded on under a jentle [gentle] brease [breeze] up the Missouri . . . to the upper Point of the lst

Island . . . camped on the island which is opposite the mouth of a Small Creek called Cold Water . . . a heavy rain this afternoon.

At this stage, the expedition included fourteen soldiers, Kentucky volunteers, and several rivermen. The rivermen were skilled in handling the boats.

York, Clark's slave, was another member of the expedition. Clark called York "my servant."

George Drouillard was probably the most valuable member of the party. He was highly skilled as a hunter and trapper. He was a crack shot.

Drouillard could speak two Native American languages. He was also an expert in sign language.

Lewis and Clark had trouble spelling Drouillard's name. They wrote it down the way it sounded to them. In their journals, Drouillard is always Drewyer.

Private Pierre Cruzatte was also highly valued. He could speak the language of the Omaha. He also knew sign language.

Playing the fiddle was another of Cruzatte's skills. In the evening, when the explorers camped,

The explorers' Wood River camp no longer exists. This Lewis and Clark Memorial in Hartford, Illinois, near the Wood River site, now marks the starting point of the expedition.

Cruzatte sometimes entertained the men with his fiddle playing.

The expedition also included Lewis's dog, Seaman. Seaman was a powerful Newfoundland with a black coat. The dog was the expedition's only pet.

Seaman was more than Lewis's companion. He served the expedition as a hunter. Seaman caught squirrels and geese. A strong swimmer, Seaman would sometimes be sent into the water to force beavers out of their homes. The men found roasted beaver tongue to be delicious to eat.

Throughout the journey, the captains kept strict discipline. Lewis and Clark realized that there would be times when their lives depended on each man doing what he had been instructed to do. Anyone who broke the rules was quickly punished.

The Missouri was a never-ending challenge. The rushing current made for hard poling. But that was only part of it. There were dangers at every turn.

In shallow spots, the men waded beside the boat. Some used ropes to pull the boat. Others pushed from the rear.

Ridges of sand in the river, called sandbars, were another hazard. In a journal entry for May 24, 1804, Clark wrote, "The swiftness of the Current . . . Broke our Toe [tow] rope, and was nearly over Setting the boat . . . all hands jumped out on the upper side and bore on that side until the Sand washed from under the boat . . ."

Great clumps of driftwood and barely sunken logs

Sergeant Patrick Gass, a member of the expedition, kept a daily account of events. His journal was first published in 1807. A later edition, published in 1812, contained a number of hand-drawn illustrations. This one depicts the perils of boat travel on the Missouri River.

also caused problems for the boats. Sometimes it would take hours for the men to fight through the debris.

As they labored with the boats, mosquitoes, gnats, and ticks assaulted the men. They suffered from stomachaches and a variety of infections. On June 17, Clark wrote, "The party is much aflicted [afflicted] with Boils, and several have Deassentary [dysentery], which I contribute to the water."

The explorers' poor diet also contributed to their poor health. Seldom did the men have fresh fruits or vegetables.

Surprisingly, only one member of the expedition died during the long journey. That was Sergeant Charles Floyd. Lewis described Floyd as having "bilious colic." What Floyd probably had was appendicitis. The captains were helpless in attempting to treat appendicitis.

Despite the problems, the explorers made steady progress. Although there were some days that they would travel only five or six miles, they also had good days. These usually came when the wind was at their backs and they could hoist their sails. On such days, it was possible to cover as much as twenty miles. Once or twice, they journeyed even farther.

Each evening, after the party had established a campsite, the men would cook and eat together. Sometimes the men would be given cornmeal and lard. Other times, it would be pork and flour.

Fortunately, the banks of the river were rich in

Sergeant Charles Floyd was the only American to die during the expedition. This 100-foot memorial in Sioux City, Iowa, marks his burial place.

game. Drouillard and the other hunters would bring back deer, turkey, and geese. They also tracked down bear and elk.

Some of the meat was "jerked." It would be cut and pounded into thin slices. These were dried in the sun. Jerked meat could be carried in one's pocket and eaten as a snack food.

On rare occasions, the expedition passed traders and trappers headed downstream to St. Louis. Their canoes would be piled high with furs and buffalo grease. They also carried tallow, an animal fat used in making candles or soap.

On June 12, the party came upon Pierre Dorion, a French-Canadian trapper. Dorion had lived among the Yankton Sioux and spoke their language as well as French and English. The captains hired Dorion as an interpreter. He agreed to stay with the party as they traveled through Sioux country.

On the evening of July 4, the expedition pulled in for the night at the site of what had been a Native American town. They could not help but be impressed by the beauty of the land. "We Camped in the plain," Clark wrote, "one of the most butifull [beautiful] Plains I ever Saw, open and butifully [beautifully] diversified with hills and vallies [valleys] all presenting them to the river, covered with grass and a few scattering trees, a handsome creek meandering thro [through]."

At sunset, the captains ordered the expedition's cannon to be fired. It was without a doubt the first Fourth of July celebration west of the Mississippi.

TROUBLES WITH
THE SIOUX

THE EXPLORERS HAD YET TO SEE A
Native American. But trappers they met
told them that once they traveled
beyond the Platte River they would come upon
the Oto and the Missouri people.

The expedition reached the meeting point of
the Missouri and Platte rivers on July 21, 1804.
They were now about one hundred miles beyond
the southern border of the present state of Iowa.

On July 30, Clark wrote of a strange animal
that had been killed and brought into camp by
Private Joseph Field. "...his Shape and Size is
like that of a Beaver," Clark wrote, his head and
mouth "like a Dog's, with Short Ears, his Tail and

Hair is like that of a Ground Hog..." The animal that Clark described was a badger.

At sunset on August 2, fourteen Oto and Missouri arrived at the expedition's camp. They came with a French guide who spoke their language. The men were cautious.

Clark wrote in his journal:

Capt. Lewis & myself met those Indians & informed them we were glad to see them, and would speak to them tomorrow. Sent them some roasted meat, pork, flour & meal . . . in return they sent us Watermillions [watermelons]. Every man on Guard and ready for any thing.

The next morning, the captains met with the Oto and the Missouri leaders on a bluff overlooking the river. They wore their full-dress uniforms. A squad of soldiers, also in full uniform, paraded.

Lewis then spoke. He explained that the Missouri River country no longer belonged to France or Spain, but to the United States. He said that all those living in that region "are bound to obey the great chief, the President, who is now your only great father." He invited the Oto and the Missouri to visit their Great Father, Thomas Jefferson, in Washington.

After Lewis's speech, the captains gave out peace medals. Then the Oto leaders spoke. They said they were happy with their new father.

The council ended on friendly terms. Clark noted that the meeting site would be a good location for a fort and a trading post. They named the site

Lewis in his dress uniform and Clark in a top hat meet with a group of Native Americans. This illustration is from Patrick Gass's journal.

Councile Bluff. It is located near the present town of Fort Calhoun, Nebraska.

Much later, the city of Council Bluffs, Iowa, was established. It is about twenty-five miles downriver from the site where Lewis and Clark had met with the Oto and the Missouri chiefs.

In the months that Lewis and Clark spent preparing for their expedition, they kept hearing fearful tales about the Sioux. They were said to be warlike people. They often took part in bloody battles with other Native Americans.

White traders had long been bullied by the Sioux. Many traders would no longer travel up the Missouri to deal with them. In the sign language of the day, the motion for Sioux was to draw one's forefinger across one's throat.

Yet Lewis and Clark knew that they could not attempt to avoid the Sioux. President Jefferson wanted Lewis and Clark to establish friendly relations with the Sioux. He wanted them to prepare the way for American traders.

On August 27, the explorers reached what is now

Yankton, South Dakota. The captains learned that there were bands of Sioux in the area. They sent Dorion and two other members of the party to invite the Sioux to meet with them. Two days later, Dorion returned. He brought with him five Sioux chiefs and seventy warriors.

These were Yankton Sioux, who turned out to be peaceful. At the council meeting a few days later, they listened patiently to Lewis's speech and accepted the medals and other gifts.

As the expedition continued up the river, trees along the banks became fewer. But they saw much more animal life. Lewis was amazed by the "immence [immense] herds of buffaloe [buffalo]..." The great masses of these animals stretched as far as the eye could see, darkening the plains.

On September 5, the men sighted what they thought to be a strange-looking goat. It was, Lewis noted, "...very actively made...his brains in the back of his head..." The animal was later determined to be a pronghorn antelope, an animal

Sioux warriors pursue stampeding buffalo. This illustration is from a painting by American artist George Catlin, who recorded the appearance and customs of Native Americans.

new to science. One was shot and stuffed to be sent back east.

On the evening of September 23, after a successful day of travel, the explorers stopped for the night. They made their camp in a grove of cottonwood trees not far from the river's edge. They had not been there very long when someone spotted three young men swimming toward the riverbank.

The pronghorn antelope, an animal discovered by the explorers during the summer of 1805

They were Teton Sioux. The Tetons were believed to be the most troublesome of all the bands of Sioux. Using sign language, Drouillard was able to exchange information with them. They reported that a large number of Sioux were camped not far upriver (near where the city of Pierre, South Dakota, now stands).

Lewis and Clark gave the young men some tobacco to take back to their leaders. They asked them to tell their chiefs that they would like to meet with them the next day.

An island in the Bad River was decided upon as a site for the meeting. The explorers set up a pole with an American flag and strung an awning to shield the group from the sun. The cautious captains gave orders that the keelboat was to be anchored offshore. Its cannon was pointed directly toward the meeting site.

At around eleven o'clock in the morning, fifty or sixty Teton warriors arrived. Three chiefs—Black Buffalo, the Partisan, and Buffalo Medicine—led them.

The warriors presented a big piece of buffalo meat as a gift. The captains gave the Tetons some pork. Lewis then delivered his speech about the Great Father in Washington.

The gift-giving that followed led to trouble. Lewis presented a medal, a colorful military coat, and a military hat to Black Buffalo. To the Partisan he gave only a medal and some knives. The Partisan felt that Black Buffalo had gotten better gifts. He got very angry.

The captains invited the chiefs aboard the keelboat. The Teton Sioux then became troublesome. The Partisan refused to go ashore.

Clark and several of the men managed to get the Partisan and the other chiefs into one of the pirogues. They then rowed them to the riverbank. When the boat landed, three warriors grabbed the bowline and prevented the boat from leaving.

That was enough for Clark. He would not let himself be bullied. He drew his sword and ordered his men to take up their arms. On board the keelboat, Lewis saw what was happening. He ordered the cannon loaded. He lit a long wick and held it just above the fuse that would fire the cannon. At the same time, the men on the keelboat put their rifles to their shoulders, pointed them toward the Tetons, and sighted down the barrels.

The Tetons were quick to react. Arrows were drawn from quivers. Bows were strung. It was a tense

This painting of a Sioux village was created by artist George Catlin around 1832.

moment. Black Buffalo acted. Seizing the bowline from the warriors, he released the pirogue.

An explosive moment had passed without bloodshed. Clark immediately tried to act as a peacemaker. He walked over to the Partisan and Buffalo Medicine and put out his hand. But the chiefs refused to take it.

Lewis and Clark spent four days among the Teton

Sioux. When they were getting ready to leave, a great number of Teton warriors appeared on the riverbank. But, again the explorers managed to escape an ugly incident.

Once they left the shore, a brisk wind behind them filled their sails. The boats hurried up the river. The captains felt badly that they had not been able to establish good relations with the Sioux. But at least no guns had been fired.

As the explorers pushed ahead, the men occasionally spotted bands of Sioux along the riverbank. The Sioux called out, begging for tobacco and asking the explorers to come ashore.

The boats did not stop. "We proceded [proceeded] on," Clark wrote.

WINTER CAMP

AS THE EXPLORERS CONTINUED UP the Missouri, each day brought signs of the changing season. The grassy plains turned a golden yellow. Overhead, great flocks of geese and mallard traveled south. Days were shorter, nights longer.

The expedition was nearing the present border of South Dakota and North Dakota. The party passed the remains of villages that had once been occupied by the Arikara. A once-powerful Native American nation, the Arikara had been all but wiped out by smallpox. The deadly disease had spread from one person to another. Those Arikara who had survived had often been attacked by the Teton Sioux.

The Arikara were farmers. They raised beans, squash, pumpkins, and tobacco. They also hunted buffalo.

After their troubled encounters with the Teton Sioux, the captains were nervous about meeting the Arikara. But there was no need for anxiety. The Arikara warmly welcomed the explorers.

The explorers spent several days among the tribe. In their first formal meeting with Arikara leaders, Lewis delivered his usual speech. Then the captains distributed gifts.

The chiefs listened to Lewis's speech without complaint and seemed pleased with their gifts. But what really excited them was Clark's slave, York. The Arikara had never seen a black person before. They stared at him in wonder and went up to him and rubbed his skin.

York loved being the center of attention. He teased the Arikara. He told them he had once been a wild animal and that he had been captured by Clark. He roared like a lion at the Arikara children and chased them around the village.

Clark thought that York might have gotten

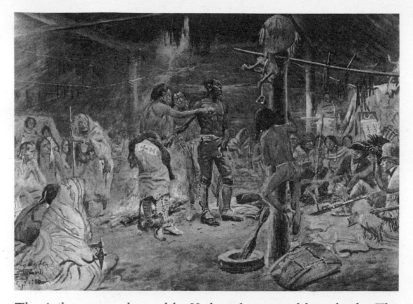

The Arikara were charmed by York and examined him closely. This scene is from a watercolor by Charles Russell, an American painter whose work often recorded the lives of Native Americans of the Great Plains.

carried away. He wrote: "... he Carried on the joke and made himself more turribal [terrible] than we wished him to doe [do]."

When the explorers left the Arikara, an Arikara chief went with them. The chief was to serve as a goodwill ambassador to the Mandan, who lived farther up the river.

The weather kept getting more winterlike. On

October 24, there were snow showers for the first time.

The same day, the explorers met their first Mandan. Chief Big White and a hunting party of twenty-five warriors greeted them in a friendly manner.

The explorers later learned that there were several thousand Native Americans living in the region. There were not only Mandan, but also Hidatsa. The Hidatsa were allies of the Mandan.

Like the Arikara, the Mandan were farming people. They had a long history of welcoming white traders and doing business with them.

The captains decided it would be wise to remain among the Mandan for the winter months. They knew that the temperatures were going to nose-dive. The river would be sure to freeze. It would be impossible to travel. The news that the explorers were to be their winter guests pleased the Mandan.

Early in November, the men set to work building the cabins they were to occupy until spring. They raised an American flag to the top of a tall pole. They called their new home Fort Mandan.

Mandan women pole their round, basin-shaped bull boats, made of buffalo hide stretched over a wooden frame. In the background, there is a Mandan village. This illustration is from a painting by Swiss-born artist Karl Bodmer, who traveled up the Missouri River in 1833.

It was bitterly cold that fall and winter. It was much colder than the men had ever experienced.

On one occasion, a hunting party was successful in killing a buffalo. But they had to leave the animal where it fell and hurry back to the fort to warm themselves. One mid-December day, their thermometer read 45 degrees below zero.

The extreme cold did not stop Lewis and Clark from operating Fort Mandan as if it were in a battle

Mandan and Hidatsa lived in large circular lodges made of wooden beams covered with earth. Each had room enough for an extended family, plus their horses. These Mandan lodges were rebuilt in Abraham Lincoln State Park near Bismarck, North Dakota.

zone. There were frequent drills and daily inspections of weapons. Guards were posted day and night.

The captains were not fearful of the Mandan. But the Teton Sioux were not a great distance away. It was always possible that they would stage a raid.

While the captains remained suspicious of the Sioux, they were always on the best of terms with the Mandan. Often the captains and their men were guests in the homes of the Native Americans.

The Mandan were smart and experienced traders. Their villages were central marketplaces for the region.

A number of white traders lived among the Native Americans. One was Toussaint Charbonneau, a French-Canadian trader. Charbonneau lived among the Hidatsa.

During the time he lived with the Hidatsas, Charbonneau had two wives. Both were Shoshone.

The Shoshone were a band of Native Americans that lived far up the Missouri in the Rocky Mountains. The Hidatsa had captured the two women several years before. At the time, they were no more than eleven or twelve.

It was agreed that one of Charbonneau's wives would be permitted to go with him when the expedition left their winter camp. Her name was Sacagawea, which meant Bird Woman. She was expecting a baby.

Lewis fully realized that having a pregnant woman as a member of the expedition could cause problems. But he also knew that Sacagawea could be very valuable to the party. She was a Shoshone. She could serve as a translator when the explorers reached the Rocky Mountains and her people.

Later that winter, Sacagawea's baby was born at Fort Mandan. The baby, a boy, was named Jean Baptiste Charbonneau. Clark nicknamed the child "Pompey," or "Pomp."

INTO THE
UNKNOWN

URING THE FIRST MONTHS OF THEIR journey, the captains had maps to follow. They also had gotten advice from white traders who had traveled the Missouri.

But once the expedition left Fort Mandan, it would be different. Lewis and Clark would be entering lands known only to Native Americans.

The explorers had gotten some help from the Hidatsa before they left Fort Mandan. The Hidatsa had told them that they would need horses to cross the mountains. There was no other way. Horses, they said, could be bought from the Shoshone.

As the explorers set out upstream, a squad of

soldiers and rivermen would return downstream in the keelboat. Packed into the keelboat were nine boxes of items for President Jefferson. These included the skins, skeletons, horns, and antlers of many of the animals that the explorers had come upon. There was even a live prairie dog.

In a report he had prepared for the president, Lewis wrote that he expected to reach the Pacific that summer. He was hopeful that the expedition might be able to return to Fort Mandan for the winter of 1805 to 1806. He said to Jefferson, "You may therefore expect to see me in Monachello [Monticello, the name of Jefferson's plantation] in September 1806."

Once the explorers were underway, they found the river to be their enemy. Because of sandbars and the strong current, the men often had to push the boats. That meant wading in freezing water that was shoulder deep.

Sometimes the river bottom was thick with mud. The men had to slog their way through. Other times

Clark's sketch of the expedition's keelboat

the bottom was covered with sharp stones that cut into their moccasins.

Using towropes, the men had to haul the boats upstream from the shore.

It was always cold. Even in May, snow fell and ice formed at night in their kettles and saucepans. Clark's journal entry for May 2, 1805, reads: "A verry extraodernarey [extraordinary] climate, to behold the trees green and flowers spred on the plains, & snow an inch deep."

Fortunately, there was plenty to eat. Day after day, the explorers sighted herds of deer, elk, and buffalo.

There was one animal they did not hunt. That was the grizzly bear. The Hidatsa had warned the captains that the grizzly was a fierce animal with great strength. This made the explorers curious. "The men as well as ourselves are anxious to meet with these bear," Lewis wrote.

One day not long after the expedition had crossed from the present state of North Dakota into Montana, they got their wish. Lewis and one of the soldiers were walking along the riverbank when they spotted two grizzlies. Each man quickly fired and hit a bear. One of the wounded animals ran off. The other charged Lewis, who turned and fled.

The wounded bear could not keep pace. That gave Lewis time to reload and shoot again. The soldier fired, too. Together, they managed to kill the animal.

On May 26, 1805, Lewis climbed low hills along

the riverbank and from them caught his first glimpse of the snow-covered Rocky Mountains far in the distance. He wrote that he felt a "secret pleasure" at finding himself so close to the source of the Missouri River. At the same time, he reflected on the "difficulties this snowy barrier would probably throw in my way" and the "sufferings and hardships" that were to come.

On June 3, 1805, the explorers came upon a fork in the river that confused them.

"An interesting question was now to be determined," wrote Lewis. "Which of these rivers is the Missouri?"

Making the right choice was vital. A chief goal of the expedition was to trace the Missouri to its source. If the explorers took the wrong branch of the river, they could end up wasting valuable weeks of travel time.

The northern branch of the river was brown and muddy like the Missouri. Most of the men felt certain that the northern branch was the right one.

Lewis and Clark did not agree. They believed that

the south fork was the one they should follow. Because it was clear and had a clean, stony bottom, it seemed obvious that it had come from a distant mountain source.

The captains explored the two streams. That made them more certain than ever that the south fork was part of the Missouri.

Lewis was so sure that the north branch was not the Missouri that he gave it a name. He called it Maria's River after a cousin back home. It has that name today (but without the apostrophe).

Their goal now was to follow the south fork until they came to the Great Falls of the Missouri. The waterfalls had been described to them by the Hidatsa at Fort Mandan.

The captains decided to split up. On June 11, Lewis set out overland to find the falls. Clark stayed behind with most of the men and the boats. Two days later, Lewis was the first to reach the Great Falls. He heard the falls before he saw them. His journal entry for June 13 reads:

. . . my ears were saluted with the agreeable sound of a fall of water and advancing a little further I saw the spray arise above the plain like a collumn [column] of smoke. . . .

There could be no doubt now. The captains had chosen the right river to follow. Lewis described the falls as a "...sublimely grand spectacle...the grandest sight I had ever beheld..."

While the falls were a natural wonder of startling beauty, they also presented a great problem. Lewis soon found that there was not one "great falls." That's

Even today, the Great Falls of the Missouri are no place for small boats.

what he had been told by the Hidatsa. Instead there were five of them. They were linked by stretches of the river in which the water ran very fast.

It was clear that the explorers would have to abandon the river and travel by foot. They would have to travel overland almost eighteen miles. The terrain was steep and rocky, with thick patches of prickly pear cactus.

The men set to work building a pair of four-wheeled wagons to carry their canoes and supplies. Lewis called them "trucks."

Not long after sunrise on June 22, 1805, the trip around the Great Falls began. It was backbreaking work. The men were pounded with cold rain and hailstones the size of eggs. Big gnats and mosquitoes pestered them. They had to grasp rocks and clumps of grass in hauling the wagons up the steep slopes. The cactus cut their feet. The cottonwood wheels cracked and split. Long stops had to be made for repairs. Lewis noted that the men became so exhausted that at "every halt, [they] are asleep in a moment..."

The men had to make four trips overland in order to carry their six large dugout canoes around the falls.

By the Fourth of July, the explorers had completed their difficult trek around the Great Falls. Now they could put their canoes back in the water again.

In the evening, they paused to celebrate the nation's twenty-ninth birthday. Cruzatte played the fiddle. The men, wrote Lewis, "...continued their mirth with songs and festive jokes and were extremely merry untill late at night."

MEETING THE SHOSHONES

THE DAYS OF HARD TRAVEL BY LAND were over. The explorers looked forward to being on the water again.

They were now traveling mostly north, with mountains on both sides. The going was seldom easy. The river had become much narrower and the current ran very fast.

On July 19, 1805, the explorers came upon an awesome canyon, three miles long. The Missouri flowed silently and swiftly through the gorge. Cliffs rose as high as 1,400 feet on each side. Lewis called the site the "Gates of the Mountains."

The boats could not be towed. There was no

Lewis named this Missouri River canyon the "Gates of the Mountains."

shoreline to provide footing for the men. The boats could not be poled, either. The water was too deep. The men had no choice but to paddle against the strong current. They had to strain every muscle to keep the boats moving.

The captains were eager to meet the Shoshone. From the Shoshone, they hoped to gain the guides and horses that would take them across the Rockies.

But the Shoshone were timid people. They were

fearful of their warlike neighbors, the Blackfoot and the Hidatsa. The Shoshone lived in the high mountains because of this warfare.

When the explorers camped, they saw fresh horse tracks and abandoned camps. They knew they were in Shoshone territory. But they saw no Shoshone.

Sacagawea was now close to her homeland. She began to point out familiar landmarks. She told the captains that they were nearing a place where the Missouri River split into three branches. Not long after, her prediction came true. The expedition came upon what is now known as the Three Forks of the Missouri.

The explorers followed the southwest branch of the three rivers. Lewis named it Jefferson's River. The stream kept getting narrower and shallower. Its banks were rocky and steep. Sacagawea said that a pass in the mountains ahead would lead them to her people.

Lewis was getting more and more eager to meet the Shoshone. He organized a search party made up of himself, Drouillard, John Shields, and Hugh

McNeal. He planned on combing the countryside until they came upon a band of Shoshone.

On August 12, the party followed the course of a small stream known as Prairie Creek. When they came to its source, Lewis believed that at last they had reached the headwaters of the Missouri River, "in search of which," he wrote, "we have spent so many toilsome days and wristless [restless] nights."

Lewis, in finding what he believed to be the source of the Missouri River, had achieved one of the expedition's chief goals. But any joy he felt must have faded quickly. As he gazed out toward the awesome mountain range to the west, he must have realized that there was no Northwest Passage. No rivers crossed the Northwest. The Rockies stood as a great barrier. Lewis perhaps felt sad that he would have to report this fact to President Jefferson.

The men continued up a gentle rise that led to a gap in the mountains. They then followed a Native American trail that continued up and through the pass. Descending the other side, they came upon a fast-running cold-water creek that was flowing westward. "Here," Lewis wrote, "I first tasted the water of the great Columbia River."

Lewis was mistaken. He had come over what is now known as the Lemhi Pass, on the border between the present states of Montana and Idaho. The stream from which he drank was the Lemhi River, not the Columbia. The waters of the Lemhi, however, eventually do reach the Columbia.

There could be no mistaking the fact that the pass

Lewis and Clark's route took them through this rugged terrain near the Montana-Idaho border.

marked the western edge of the Louisiana Territory. As the explorers headed west, they would no longer be in the United States. They would be traveling in the Oregon Territory.

On the morning of August 13, 1805, Lewis woke up early. He set out again with Drouillard, McNeal, and Shields. They followed a Native American trail that led into a long valley.

They had covered about ten miles when they came upon three Shoshone. One was a girl of about twelve and another was a teenage girl. The third was an elderly woman.

Lewis put his rifle on the ground. Then he walked toward the group. The teenager ran off. The younger girl and the older woman stayed. They sat down on the ground before Lewis and lowered their heads. It was as if they expected to die.

Lewis took the elderly woman by the hand and raised her to her feet. He rolled up his sleeve and pointed to his white skin. "*Ta-ba-bone,*" he said. The phrase meant "white man."

The explorers reached into their sacks and took

out beads and mirrors and other gifts. The woman and young girl became calm.

Drouillard, using sign language, asked the woman to call back the teenager. When she rejoined the group, Lewis gave her several gifts.

Lewis then applied dabs of red paint to the cheeks of the woman and the two girls. Sacagawea had told Lewis that this was a sign of peace. The red paint worked. The Shoshone now seemed completely relaxed.

Drouillard, again using sign language, asked the three to lead them to their camp. He explained that they wanted to meet their chiefs and warriors.

On the way, the explorers were startled by the sudden approach of some sixty or so warriors on horseback. Most of them were armed with bows and arrows. A few had rifles.

When he saw the Shoshone warriors, Lewis put down his rifle and picked up a flag. He walked slowly toward them. One of the warriors rode ahead of the others. Lewis believed that he might be their chief. The elderly woman went up to him, spoke excitedly, and showed him the gifts she had been given.

The tension melted. The chief and two other men got down from their horses and walked up to Lewis. In his journal, Lewis explained what happened next:

. . . these men then . . . embraced me very affectionately in their way, which is by putting their left arm over your wright [right] shoulder [and] clasping your back, while they apply their left cheek to yours . . .

At the same time, the Shoshone kept repeating, "*ah-hi-e, ah-hi-e.*" Lewis later learned the word meant, "I am much pleased." In the Shoshone camp, Lewis met Cameahwait, the Shoshone chief. Seated in the chief's tipi, they smoked the pipe of peace.

Clark, meanwhile, was traveling up Jefferson's River with the other members of the expedition. After Clark arrived at the Shoshone village, Lewis called for a meeting with Cameahwait and the other Shoshone leaders. Sacagawea was brought in to act as the interpreter.

After she had taken her seat, Sacagawea began to stare at Cameahwait. Suddenly she recognized him

Congress passed a law in 1999 that provided for the minting of a new dollar coin bearing Sacagawea's image. The coin is gold-colored and depicts an eagle on the reverse side. These were the proposed designs for the coin.

as her brother. Sacagawea jumped to her feet, ran to him, and threw her arms around the chief. Then she began crying. When the meeting began again, Sacagawea was probably so filled with joy that she broke into tears from time to time.

Cameahwait began the meeting by saying that his people were very poor. Often they went hungry. They needed guns for hunting and fighting off their enemies.

Lewis answered that they had no guns to give them now. He made it clear, however, that his government would later provide them with the weapons they needed. But this could not happen until Lewis returned home. He asked Cameahwait and his leaders to help in making their journey a rapid one by providing them with guides and horses.

Cameahwait took this news well. As Lewis wrote,

The chief thanked us for [our] friendship . . . and declared his wish to serve us in every rispect [respect] . . . [and] that he would encourage his people to come over with their horses and that he would bring his own and assist us.

Lewis and Clark bought twenty-nine horses from the Shoshone. That meant that almost every member of the expedition would have a horse for the days to come.

CHAPTER 10

CROSSING THE ROCKIES

WHAT WAS TO BE THE MOST difficult part of the long journey loomed just ahead. The explorers would be crossing the Bitterroot Mountains. The Bitterroots, in Idaho, are part of the Rocky Mountain chain.

In the Bitterroots, the explorers entered a great maze of snow-covered ridges and passes. It was country harsher and more hazardous than any they had faced before. Even today, few people live there.

The captains had persuaded the Shoshone to provide them with a guide. They called him Old Toby.

Besides the rough terrain, the explorers had to cope with below-freezing temperatures. Winter came early in the Bitterroots. On August 26, the temperature hit the freezing mark. On September 3, it snowed.

Clark's journal entry for September 3 gives some idea of the troubles they faced. He wrote:

> *. . . hills high and rocky on each side . . . horses could scurcely [scarcely] keep from slipping down . . . several sliped [slipped] and injured themselves verry much . . . little to eate [eat] . . . snow about two inches deep when it began to rain . . ."*

The next day, the explorers met a band of friendly Salish. The Salish were on good terms with the Shoshone. They were pleased to meet Old Toby.

The captains smoked pipes of peace with the Salish. They also bought thirteen horses and "a few articles of merchandize [merchandise]" from them.

Over the next three days, the explorers descended into a wide and beautiful valley. Beyond the valley they could see the snow-covered Bitterroots. Sergeant

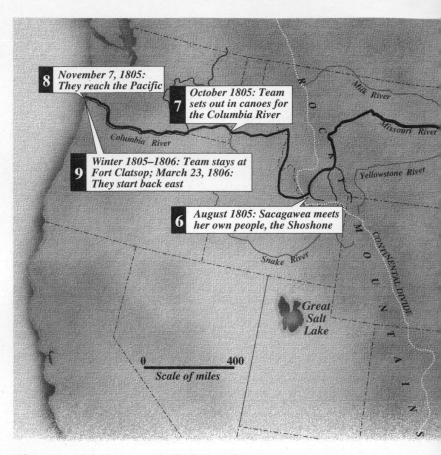

The route of the Lewis and Clark Expedition

Patrick Gass described them as "the most terrible mountains I ever beheld..."

On the night of September 9, the expedition camped not far from the Bitterroot River at the

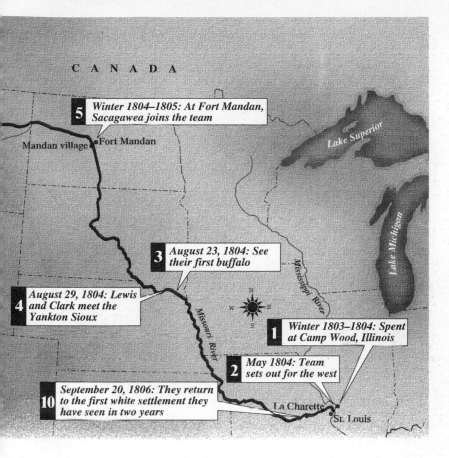

CANADA

5 Winter 1804–1805: At Fort Mandan, Sacagawea joins the team

Mandan village Fort Mandan

Lake Superior

Lake Michigan

3 August 23, 1804: See their first buffalo

4 August 29, 1804: Lewis and Clark meet the Yankton Sioux

Mississippi River

Missouri River

1 Winter 1803–1804: Spent at Camp Wood, Illinois

2 May 1804: Team sets out for the west

10 September 20, 1806: They return to the first white settlement they have seen in two years

La Charette St. Louis

mouth of a stream that joined the river from the west. Today, that stream is known as Lolo Creek. Lewis decided to pause for a day and rest their horses. He called their campsite Traveler's Rest.

Before leaving, Lewis sent out the party's hunters. He wanted to stock up on deer, beaver, and other kinds of game before the expedition got deep into the mountains.

On September 11, 1805, the explorers set out across the Bitterroots. They kept to the present Lolo Trail. Ten days of misery followed.

Snow covered the ground. Fallen timber blocked their path. Horses slipped and fell. "Party and horses much fatigued," Clark wrote after only two days of travel.

Game was scarce. But on September 13, the hunters managed to kill some pheasants and a deer.

On September 14, it rained and hailed in the valleys. In the mountains, it snowed. Clark described the trail as "much worse than yesterday."

The explorers' food supply gave out. They had no choice but to kill and eat one of their horses.

The next day was worse. Going up a steep and winding mountain trail, several horses slipped and tumbled down the mountain. The horse carrying Clark's portable desk was one of those that fell. The desk went speeding down the mountain until it smashed into a tree. The mishap "broke the desk," as Clark noted, "[but] the horse escaped and appeared but little hurt."

When the explorers reached the summit, there was no water to be found and there was scarcely any food. Using melted snow, the cooks made a soup out of the remains of the colt that they had killed the day before.

On September 16, the suffering continued. It began snowing three hours before daybreak and continued snowing all day. Clark, walking in front of the party, had great difficulty keeping on the trail. He shivered in the cold. "I have been wet and as cold in every part as I ever was in my life," he wrote. "I was at one time fearful my feet would freeze in the thin Mockirsons [moccasins] which I wore."

The captains decided it would be best if the expedition split up. Clark would go ahead with six hunters. Whenever they found and shot game, they would send it back to the main party.

The first night out, Clark and his party camped

near a stream. Clark named it Hungery [hungry] Creek because "at that place we had nothing to eate [eat]."

On the second day out, Clark and his hunters descended into a valley. There they came upon a village near the present Weipee, Idaho. The village was populated by the Chopponish.

The Chopponish were a much larger nation than the Shoshone. They had never had any contact with white men. They could easily have killed Clark and his near-starving group. After holding a council, they decided they would not. Instead, speaking in sign language, they offered the explorers their friendship.

The Chopponish served Clark dried salmon and flour made from the root of

In the Northwest, Native Americans and explorers alike lived on a diet of fish, mostly salmon. This is Clark's drawing of the white trout salmon.

a lilylike plant called the camas. The men feasted. That night they got upset stomachs from overeating.

A few days later, Lewis and his men arrived at the Chopponish village. They were exhausted. Lewis himself was so weak that he could not support himself in the saddle.

Lewis and his men gobbled down the Chopponish food just as Clark and his party had. They, too, got very sick.

Lewis remained ill for more than a week. He was unable to smoke a ceremonial pipe. He couldn't give his speech about the Great Father in Washington. Clark did these things for him.

Twisted Hair, the Chopponish chief, drew a map for Clark on white elk skin. It showed the land to the west. According to what Twisted Hair said, they were not far from the Clearwater River. The Clearwater flowed west to join the Columbia River.

Clark put the men to work cutting down ponderosa pine trees to make canoes. This time Clark and his men used the Native American method of canoe making. Instead of hollowing out the trunks with axes, they burned them out. It took ten days to create five canoes.

Before leaving the Chopponish village, Clark ordered the expedition's thirty-eight horses to be rounded up. Each was branded with a hot iron that read CAPT. M. LEWIS. Then the horses were turned over to the Chopponish. They promised to look after them until the explorers returned on their homeward journey.

On October 7, 1805, the men launched their canoes into the Clearwater River. Twisted Hair, along with another Chopponish leader named Tetoharsky, volunteered to serve as their guides until they reached the Columbia River.

They were headed downstream now. They knew that they still had a good distance to travel. They knew the swift-flowing river was filled with dangerous rapids. But such things hardly mattered now. Their goal was in sight.

CHAPTER 11

TO THE PACIFIC

THE CAPTAINS' GOAL NOW WAS TO reach the Pacific Ocean. Once they had done that, they could decide where to spend the winter. They could begin their return journey to St. Louis when the winter had passed.

As their dugout canoes made their way down the Clearwater River, the explorers often traveled at great speed. But they faced one hazard after another. The boats hit rocks. They sprung leaks.

Yet the captains had no wish to travel by land. Traveling by foot and carrying the boats and their supplies would slow them down. They were eager to reach their goal.

On October 10, 1805, the explorers rode into the Snake River. The Snake joined the Clearwater

River from the south. That night the expedition camped near the site of the present Lewiston, Idaho.

Within a week, the expedition passed from the Snake River into the Columbia River. The explorers had entered the present state of Washington.

The captains bought food from the Native Americans. Mostly it was salmon. In fact, the men became bored with a diet of fish. They also bought dogs from the Native Americans to eat. Most of them preferred dog to dried salmon.

Throughout this part of the journey, the Native Americans were always friendly. Clark believed that they were friendly because of Sacagawea. "A woman with a party of men is a token of peace," Clark wrote.

The explorers continued down the river. When the expedition stopped at night, the men were greeted by Wanapam. The Native Americans entertained the explorers with dancing and singing.

About a week after the explorers entered the Columbia River, they reached the rapids above the Great Falls. The falls had a sheer drop of twenty feet. They are now known as Celilo Falls.

The canoes had to be unloaded. They were then lowered over the falls by ropes that the men had made out of elk skin.

Below the falls, where the river widened, the explorers camped for three days. They needed to repair their canoes and dry their belongings. Their campsite was near the present city of The Dalles, Oregon.

A problem developed when the men visited the Native American campsites. Their tents and lodges were infested with fleas. The fleas swarmed over the men. They could not shake them off. Once, after stopping at a campsite, Clark wrote that "every man of the party was obliged to strip naked . . . that they might have an opportunity of brushing the flees [fleas] off their legs and bodies."

On the river, the explorers moved at a brisk pace. They made thirty or more miles a day. They began to see signs that they were getting close to the Pacific Ocean. One day they saw a Native American wearing a sailor's jacket. He had no doubt gotten it from a British ship that traded for furs along the coast.

Charles Russell's dramatic painting of Lewis and Clark on the Columbia River. Sacagawea is standing.

On November 7, the day dawned with a heavy fog. But by mid-afternoon the sky cleared. Then came the moment they had all awaited. "Great joy in camp," Clark wrote. "We are in view of the Ocian [Ocean], the great Pacific Octean [Ocean] we have been so long anxious to see."

They could hear the ocean's waves breaking on the rocks. Clark also noted, "Ocian [Ocean] 4142 miles from the mouth of the Missouri River."

There was no celebration. It was raining too hard. But each man must have felt a sense of triumph. And one of relief.

When Clark declared that the explorers had reached the Pacific Ocean, he was not exactly right. What the captains had looked out upon was the wide mouth of the Columbia River. It was as much as six miles across.

The Columbia not only looked like the Pacific Ocean. It was salty and tasted like the ocean. It felt like the ocean, too. When the men tried paddling their dugout canoes in the river, they bobbed around like pieces of driftwood. Some of the men got seasick.

On November 17, 1805, Clark announced that he was setting out by foot the next day to see the "main Ocian [Ocean]." Anyone who wanted to join him should be ready to start early the next morning. Ten men agreed to go along.

Heading west from their campsite on the north bank of the Columbia, the party trudged several miles to Camp Disapointment [Disappointment]. (John Marks, a British explorer who had visited the area in 1788, had named the site.) Clark and his men climbed a hill and looked to the west. He wrote: "... [the] men appear much Satisfied with their trip beholding with estonishment [astonishment] the high waves dashing against the rocks & this emence Ocian [immense Ocean]." This time they had truly reached the Pacific Ocean.

During the next several weeks, the explorers searched for a winter campsite. After crossing to the south shore of the Columbia River, they finally found what seemed like a good spot. It was located on a small bluff overlooking the present Lewis and Clark River, about three miles from its mouth.

A nearby spring could provide fresh water. Big fir trees were all around. They could be cut down to make a fort. Native Americans had told them that the site was near good hunting grounds.

Working in the rain, the men built a log cabin stockade with several rooms. It rained almost every day. When it did not rain, the sky was overcast. On December 16, Clark wrote:

The winds violent. Trees falling in every direction, whorl winds [whirlwinds], with gusts of rain Hail & Thunder. This kind of weather lasted all day. Certainly one of the worst days that ever was!

A good number of the men became ill. Some had boils. Others suffered from dysentery. One man strained a knee. Another broke a shoulder.

Elk meat they had tried to keep went bad because it was so damp. Even their dried salmon became moldy. The men's clothing mildewed and rotted.

In a drawing from Gass's journal, the men set to work building Fort Clatsop.

By Christmas Day, 1805, work on the cabins was nearing completion. The captains gave out tobacco to those who smoked or chewed it. Those who did not use tobacco received handkerchiefs. But it was not a festive day. "Showery, wet, and disagreeable," Clark wrote.

Parties of Clatsop, the Native Americans who lived in the area, were regular visitors at the fort. At first, the explorers communicated with the Clatsop by means of sign language. But eventually Drouillard learned to speak the Chinook language, which was used by the Clatsop. Many of the men learned Chinook words and phrases.

Boredom was the chief problem at Fort Clatsop. The entry "Not any occurrences today worthy of notice" appears in Lewis's daily log over and over through January, February, and into March 1806.

It was never as cold as it had been at Fort Mandan the winter before. But at Fort Clatsop it rained. It rained almost every day. Sometimes the rain would change to snow. Then it would change back to rain again.

The captains organized groups of men into hunting parties. They were sent out daily. They brought back more than a hundred elk that winter. Deer and bear were also hunted. Sometimes the hunters picked berries for the men.

The men spent a good deal of time making clothes and footwear for their return journey. They made over 300 pairs of moccasins out of elk skin. Each member of the expedition thus had about ten pairs of moccasins. Making moccasins kept the men busy. They also made shirts and trousers for the return trip.

The captains hoped to be able to leave Fort Clatsop on March 20. But rain and violent winds made the river too rough for canoe travel. They had to postpone their departure.

Not long after noon on March 23, 1806, the explorers started out. Speaking of Fort Clatsop, Clark wrote,

At this place, we had wintered and remained from the 7th of Decr. [Dec.] 1805 to this day, and have lived

Visitors are welcome at this reconstruction of Fort Clatsop, located just south of Astoria, Oregon.

as well as we had any right to expect, and we can say that we were never one day without 3 meals of some kind, either pore [poor] Elk meat or roots."

Clark, however, complained about the rain, which, he noted, "has fallen almost constantly since we passed the long narrows."

CHAPTER 12

HOMEWARD JOURNEY

THERE WAS MORE RAIN AS THE explorers made their way up the Columbia River. From time to time, they stopped to explore the land. Their hunting parties kept ahead of the canoes, seeking elk and deer.

Paddling was hard work. The river current was very strong and there were dangerous rapids. Often the canoes had to be towed or carried.

From the moment they left Fort Clatsop, the explorers could think of little but the Rocky Mountains. They could not forget how they had suffered from cold and hunger in crossing the mountains just months before. "That wretched portion of our journey," is what Clark called it.

The explorers needed to keep moving at a rapid pace. The captains' goal was to recross the Rockies and reach the Missouri River before it froze. If they were not able to reach their goal, they would be forced to spend another winter in the wilderness. No one wanted to do that.

As the men made their way up the Columbia River, they passed some of the same Native Americans they had met while traveling west the previous year. The Native Americans welcomed the explorers as friends.

On April 1, the expedition met bands of Native Americans in canoes who were making their way downstream. These Native Americans explained that they had used up their supply of dried fish. Now they were scouting the countryside for food.

That was bad news. In the country ahead, there were no elk. There were no deer. The captains had been planning on buying dried fish from the Native Americans.

Clark's drawing of a canoe used by the Native Americans on the Columbia River. Carved heads of animals were mounted at both ends.

The captains decided to halt the expedition for a few days. Hunting parties were sent out. Elk, deer, and other game that they killed was jerked. That meat supply would have to last until they reached the Chopponish villages.

As they made their way up the river, the explorers continued to struggle against the rapids. They were near the Great Falls of the Columbia. Their equipment and supplies would have to be carried around the falls. Fortunately, they were able to buy horses from the Native Americans. The horses did the heavy carrying.

Not all the Native Americans were helpful. The Wahclellah, for example, were difficult. Clark described them as being "the greatest thieves and scoundrels we have met with."

The Wahclellah tried to steal Lewis's dog, Seaman. When Lewis learned of the attempted theft, he sent three men to try to get the dog back. If the Wahclellah resisted, the men were under orders to shoot them. Luckily, when the Wahclellah realized that they were being pursued, they left the dog and fled. The expedition later lost a robe and a saddle to the Wahclellah.

The Wahclellah did not think they were stealing from the explorers. In their culture, if you weren't making use of something, it was there for someone else to use. Lewis and Clark thought the Wahclellah were thieves, but the Wahclellah could not understand why their behavior upset the white strangers.

Farther up the river, the explorers met the Wallawalla. They were much different. They brought food and firewood to the explorers. They also gave the expedition two canoes. A Wallawalla chief presented Clark with an elegant white horse.

The explorers stayed with the Wallawalla for three days. Of the Wallawalla, Lewis wrote: "... they are the most hospitable, honest, and sincere people that we have met with in our voyage."

Leaving the Wallawalla, the explorers continued up the Columbia. Where it turned north, they left the river. They then followed an overland route to the east. They were entering Chopponish country.

The explorers set up camp along the Clearwater River near the Chopponish village. Food was in short supply.

Clark's medical skill helped to solve the food problem. He had earlier become known as a healer among the Chopponish. Now he began treating their various illnesses. In return, Clark accepted food.

Clark treated as many as fifty Chopponish a day. Sore eyes were a common ailment. There were also infections and back pain.

From their campsite, the explorers could see the snow-covered Bitterroot Mountains. Despite the dangers they knew they would encounter in crossing the mountains, the explorers were eager to get started. But the Chopponish warned them that the snow was too deep. The captains would have to wait.

A week went by, then two weeks, then three. On June 10, after almost a month of waiting, the explorers were ready to set out for the Bitterroots. Chief Twisted Hair had returned to them the horses that the captains had left in his care.

Although they were friendly with the explorers, the Chopponish did not want to provide them with guides. They feared that the Blackfoot or another hostile band would attack them.

Blackfoot horse raiders armed themselves with guns and knives. Their knives, carried in rawhide sheaths, were heavy enough to serve as axes. They were used to cut wood for overnight shelters.

For the first few days, all went well. But when the expedition reached the high country, things got difficult. The snow was still fourteen or fifteen feet deep in many places. The horses kept slipping and falling. At times, they could not find the trail. Since the grass was snow-covered there was often nothing for the horses to eat.

The captains sadly decided that they would have

to turn back. As Clark noted in his journal, "This is the first time since we have been on this tour that we have been compelled to retreat..."

The captains did not attempt to test the Bitterroots again until they could convince the Chopponish to provide them with guides. When they set out a second time, the going was easier. Lewis called the Chopponish guides "most admireable [admirable] pilots." The snow was deep, but firm.

At this point, Lewis and Clark made a fateful decision. They decided to split up. Lewis, with nine men, would take a new, shorter route to the Missouri River. From there, he would set out to explore the Marias River.

Once he had completed this mission, Lewis would wait at the mouth of the Marias. There he would meet members of the party coming down the Missouri. Sergeant John Ordway would be leading these men.

Meanwhile, Clark and other members of the expedition would set out on foot and build their canoes. They would explore the Yellowstone River. They planned to follow the Yellowstone downstream to the Missouri.

It was a risky plan. The captains were dividing the expedition into small groups just as they were entering country where the Blackfoot and other warring bands of Native Americans roamed.

On July 17, Lewis began to explore the Marias River. Perhaps it would come close to Canada's Saskatchewan River. The Marias would then be part of a route for bringing furs south out of Canada. But Lewis soon found the Marias flowed west, not north into Canada.

Lewis decided to head back. He and his men had seen many signs of Native Americans. Lewis suspected that they were not friendly. He wanted to avoid them. On July 25, 1806, he wrote: "We consider ourselves extreemly [extremely] fortunate in not having met with these people."

The next day, Lewis's good fortune changed. He saw "a very unpleasant sight"—eight Blackfoot.

Lewis decided to approach them as a friend. He invited the Blackfoot to camp with him and his men that night.

Lewis stayed up late smoking with the Blackfoot. By sign language, he told them of his close ties with the Chopponish and the Shoshone. This news alarmed the Blackfoot. Those nations were their enemies.

Lewis did not trust the Blackfoot. He worried that they might try to steal their horses. He assigned Private Reubin Field to stand guard. Then Lewis went to sleep.

Loud shouts awoke Lewis at daybreak. "Let go my gun!" he heard Drouillard yell. Drouillard was scuffling with a Blackfoot over a rifle.

Another Blackfoot had grabbed rifles belonging to Reubin Field and his brother Joseph. When the Blackfoot ran off, the Field brothers went after them and caught them. A fierce struggle followed. Reubin Field stabbed a Blackfoot with a knife.

Drouillard, meanwhile, pursued the Blackfoot

who had his rifle. After he caught him, he managed to get his rifle back without any bloodshed.

Other Blackfoot began driving off the explorers' horses. Lewis ran after them. When they stopped, Lewis shouted that he would shoot them if they did not return the horses.

One of the Blackfoot was armed with a British rifle. When he turned toward Lewis, the captain aimed and fired at the Blackfoot.

The Blackfoot fell to his knees. Still, he managed

Lewis's tragic encounter with the Blackfoot is shown in this sketch from Gass's journal. The man in the fur hat at Lewis's side may be George Drouillard, the expedition's guide and interpreter.

to raise his rifle and fire at Lewis. The bullet just missed. "Being bearheaded [bareheaded]," Lewis wrote, "I felt the wind of the bullet very distinctly."

One Blackfoot was dead. Another was dying. Lewis knew that bands of Blackfoot warriors would soon be seeking revenge. He told his men that they must take flight.

Quickly, Lewis and his men saddled their horses. They not only had their own horses. They also took four Blackfoot horses.

Lewis set out toward the Missouri River at a fast gallop. By the time it was dark, they were eighty miles from the scene of the bloody fight. They rested briefly. Traveling by moonlight, they rode on, covering another twenty or so miles.

At around two o'clock in the morning, they stopped to rest. They saddled up again at daybreak and resumed their ride.

Good luck was with them. When they reached the Missouri River, they rode down it for about eight miles. Then, as Lewis wrote, "on arriving at the bank of the river, [we] had the unspeakable satisfaction to see our canoes coming down."

It was Sergeant Ordway and his party of sixteen men. They were traveling in five canoes and had the white pirogue.

The boats pulled to shore. Lewis and his men jumped into them.

As the canoes headed downstream, Lewis must have breathed a great sigh of relief. But he surely felt disappointment as well. His plans to explore the Marias had ended in terrible violence.

During their long journey, the captains had shown remarkable ability in gaining the trust of the Native Americans. Few of the white men who were to follow would be as successful. But the explorers' tragic struggle with the Blackfoot stained their record.

CHAPTER 13

HEROES RETURN

AFTER ABOUT TWO WEEKS OF HARD paddling, Sergeant Ordway's boats carrying Lewis and his men caught up with Clark's boats. But Lewis could not celebrate. He had been seriously hurt.

The day before the captains joined forces again, Lewis and Pierre Cruzatte had gone ashore to hunt elk. During the hunt, Cruzatte accidentally shot Lewis in the seat of the pants. He had mistaken him for an elk in the dense brush.

Fortunately, the bullet missed Lewis's hipbone. But Lewis was in terrible pain. He spent the night lying belly-down in the pirogue.

Lewis could no longer write in his journal. He gave full command to Clark.

After a few more days of boat travel, Lewis and Clark reached the Mandan villages. There they had spent the winter of 1804 to 1805. The Mandan welcomed them.

During their visit, Charbonneau and Sacagawea decided to leave the expedition and stay with the Hidatsa. Clark was saddened by this news. He had grown fond of Pomp. He described Sacagawea's son as a "butifull [beautiful], promising child."

Farther down the river, the captains stopped at an Arikara village. Lewis was still in great pain from the gunshot wound. But on August 26, 1806, Clark was able to write that Lewis was "on the mending hand" and "walks a little."

As the explorers got closer to home, they met canoes carrying American traders. They learned that most people had thought they were dead. President Jefferson was one of the few who still held out hope for their return.

On September 9, the explorers passed the mouth of the Platte River. They were speeding along now. Often they traveled seventy to eighty miles in a day.

On September 20, 1806, the expedition came in sight of a tiny village on the Missouri River not far from St. Louis. The village was La Charette. It was the first white settlement that the explorers had seen in more than two years.

The next day, the expedition reached St. Charles. Everyone celebrated.

On September 23, sweeping down the Mississippi River, the explorers passed their old camp at Wood River. It was a short distance to St. Louis.

When they arrived there, it seemed as if the whole town turned out to welcome them. The lean, tanned men, dressed in worn leather clothes, were a sight to behold. A newspaper described them as "Robinson Crusoes—dressed in buckskins."

The following day, Clark made one of his final journal entries. He wrote:

I sleped [slept] but little last night. However, we rose early and commenced wrighting [writing] our letters. Capt. Lewis wrote one to the president and I wrote Govr. Harrison & my friends in Kentucky . . ."

A monument to Lewis and Clark by sculptor Charles Keck

Jefferson felt "unspeakable joy" on learning of the explorers' return. He reported to Congress that the expedition had "descended the Columbia to the Pacific Ocean . . . [and] learned the character of the country, of its commerce and its inhabitants."

The expedition produced many other successes.

In two years and four months of travel, the explorers had covered more than 8,000 miles. Much of their journey had been through unknown lands.

The explorers had set up peaceful relations with most of the Native Americans they had met. They brought back new knowledge of Native American languages and culture.

The group had discovered more than 100 animals new to science. These included the prairie dog, blacktail deer, jackrabbit, and trumpeter swan.

They had found almost 200 new types of plants. Grasses and shrubs, and fruits and flowers, were among them.

The explorers did not discover a continuous river route across the country. But their travel beyond the Missouri River did have an important benefit. The expedition enabled the United States to later claim the Oregon Territory, which became part of the United States in 1846. The vast pioneer movement quickly followed.

Lewis's and Clark's journals are another of their accomplishments. The nation's written history has few greater prizes.

CHAPTER 14

LEWIS AND CLARK REMEMBERED

THE SUCCESS OF THE EXPEDITION did not translate into happiness for Meriwether Lewis. After the explorers returned to St. Louis, he led an often-troubled life.

Lewis resigned from the army in 1807. President Jefferson then made him governor of the Louisiana Territory.

Lewis's headquarters were to be in St. Louis. He did not arrive there until March 8, 1808.

During his early months as governor, Lewis was busy and successful. He encouraged the building of roads and other improvements. He helped to bring law and order to the frontier.

But he began to have serious problems. He made some unwise investments. He seemed to be always lacking money. He borrowed from many different sources.

In the summer of 1809, Lewis received bad news from Washington. The government refused to pay for some of his expenses.

Lewis decided he would go to Washington to try to straighten out matters. He started down the Mississippi River to New Orleans. From there he planned to take a sailing ship to the nation's capital.

In mid-September 1809, Lewis's boat arrived at Chickasaw Bluffs in Tennessee, the site of the present Memphis. Lewis then decided to leave the boat and make his way overland to Washington.

He set out on horseback. Two servants went with him.

For this portrait, originally drawn in 1807, Meriwether Lewis posed in buckskins and a fancy fur cape.

On October 10, Lewis's party stopped at a log cabin that took in travelers. It was named Grinder's Inn.

During the night, a shot rang out. Then another. At daybreak, Lewis was found with bullet wounds in his head and side. He died soon after. Lewis was thirty-five years old.

Some historians believe Lewis was murdered by robbers. Others believe he took his own life.

William Clark led a much more placid life than Lewis. In 1813, Clark was appointed governor of the Missouri Territory. He was also named Superintendent of Indian Affairs.

During the War of 1812, in which the United States fought the British, Clark's job took on added importance. The British sought to arouse the Native Americans and turn them against the people of the United States. Some Native American raids took place. But Clark was able to prevent an all-out war.

Clark served as governor of the Missouri Territory until 1821, when Missouri became a state. The

Native Americans came to trust and respect him. They often visited Clark's St. Louis home.

Sacagawea and her husband also visited Clark in St. Louis. They left their son Jean Baptiste, or Pomp, with Clark. The general acted as the boy's guardian. He also arranged for Pomp's education. When Pomp grew up, he became a popular guide for Western travelers.

Charbonneau became a guide and interpreter for fur traders.

Little is known of Saca-gawea. According to a trader's journal, she died in 1812. But one of her biog-raphers claimed that she died in 1884. She was said to be living on a Shoshone reservation at the time of her death.

American artist George Catlin painted this portrait of William Clark in 1832. Clark was sixty-two years old at the time.

Clark married in 1809. He raised a family of five

children. He named his firstborn son Meriwether Lewis Clark.

After the death of his wife, Clark married again. He and his second wife had two children.

Clark died in St. Louis in 1838. His funeral was said to be the most impressive that had ever taken place in that city.

After Lewis and Clark had completed their journey, they believed the trail they had mapped to the Pacific would become a busy trading route. They were wrong about that. Far easier ways were found of getting to the Pacific coast.

But Lewis and Clark and their trail have not been forgotten. Far from it.

You can now explore much of the route traveled by Lewis and Clark. You can follow in their footsteps.

In 1978, Congress established the Lewis and Clark National Historic Trail. It follows the route traveled by the explorers. It begins near Wood River, Illinois. From that site on May 14, 1804, the explorers launched their expedition. The trail makes its way up the Missouri River, then through

Hikers along the Lewis and Clark Trail in Rocheport, Missouri

South Dakota and North Dakota. It crosses into Montana and Idaho. It then follows the Columbia River to Fort Clatsop near Astoria, Oregon. The trail covers 3,700 miles.

State and local agencies and private organizations manage sections of the trail. Along the way, there are exhibitions, museums, and visitors' centers.

Some portions of the trail can be covered on foot. Others are for travel by bicycle or on horseback.

Sections of the trail along the Missouri and Columbia rivers can be traveled by boat.

Some travelers prefer to explore the route by automobile. Modern roads follow the trail in many areas.

There is a wide assortment of historic sites along the trail. You can visit what is now called Decision Point in Loma, Montana. Here the Missouri River meets the Marias River. At Decision Point, Lewis and Clark had to choose which river was actually the Missouri.

You can take a boat tour to view the Gates of the Mountains in west central Montana. Here the Missouri River knifes its way through a canyon three miles long. Towering cliffs loom on each side.

There are even hiking and horseback trails over the Lolo Trail in Idaho. This is the trail that Lewis and Clark used in crossing the rugged Bitterroot Mountains.

In two hundred years, much has changed along the Lewis and Clark Trail. Rivers have been

This memorial plaque has been placed at Decision Point near Loma, Montana, the meeting point of the Missouri and Marias rivers.

dammed. Forests have been cut. Busy cities have sprung up. Blacktopped roads stretch to the horizon.

But traces of the wilderness still exist. In many places, you can look out at the land and rivers and see just what Lewis and Clark saw some two hundred years ago.

CHRONOLOGY

1770   William Clark is born.

1774   Meriwether Lewis is born.

1775   American Revolution begins.

1776   Congress adopts the Declaration of Independence.

1783   Treaty of Paris ends the Revolutionary War.

1800   Thomas Jefferson is elected President.

1801   Lewis becomes Jefferson's private secretary.

1803   U. S. purchases Louisiana Territory from France.

1804   The Lewis and Clark Expedition begins.
President Jefferson is reelected.
Expedition spends winter at Fort Mandan.

1805   Expedition reaches Pacific Ocean.

1806   Expedition starts homeward journey.
Expedition reaches St. Louis.

1807   Lewis becomes Governor of the Louisiana Territory.
Clark becomes Brigadier General for the Louisiana
Territory.

1809   Meriwether Lewis dies.

1813   Clark becomes governor of the Missouri Territory.

1814   Lewis's and Clark's journals are first published.

1838   William Clark dies.

1904   Complete journals published in eight volumes.

1978   Congress establishes the Lewis and Clark National
Historic Trail.

2004   Bicentennial celebration of Lewis and Clark
Expedition begins.

BIBLIOGRAPHY

Primary Sources

Coues, Elliot, editor. *The History of the Louis and Clark Expedition*. New York: Dover ed., 1987; reprint of 1893 Francis P. Harper four-volume ed., 1893.

DeVoto, Bernard, editor. *Journals of Lewis and Clark*. New York: Houghton Mifflin, 1997.

Gass, Patrick. *A Journal of the Voyages and Travels of a Corps of Discovery Under the Command of Capt. Lewis and Capt. Clark*. Minneapolis: Ross and Haines, 1958.

Jackson, Donald, editor. *Letters of the Lewis and Clark Expedition with Related Documents: 1783–1854* 2nd ed. Urbana: University of Illinois Press, 1978.

Thwaites, Reuben Gold, editor. *Original Journals of the Lewis and Clark Expedition*. New York: Arno Press reprint, 1969.

Secondary Sources

Ambrose, Stephen E. *Undaunted Courage: Meriwether Lewis, Thomas Jefferson, and the Opening of the American West*. New York: Touchstone Press, 1996.

Ambrose, Stephen E. *Voyage of Discovery*. Washington, D.C.: The National Geographic Society, 1998.

Burroughs, Raymond. *The Natural History of the Lewis and Clark Expedition*. East Lansing, Michigan: Michigan State University Press, 1961.

Clark, Ella Elizabeth. *Sacagawea of the Lewis and Clark Expedition*. Berkeley: University of California Press, 1979.

Dillon, Richard. *Meriwether Lewis: A Biography*. New York: Coward-McCann, 1965.

Duncan, Dayton and Ken Burns. *Lewis & Clark: The Journey of the Corps of Discovery*. New York: Alfred A. Knopf, 1997.

Hawke, David Freeman. *Those Tremendous Mountains: The Story of the Lewis and Clark Expedition.* New York: Norton, 1980.

Ronda, James P. *Lewis and Clark Among the Indians.* Lincoln: University of Nebraska Press, 1984.

Satterfield, Archie. *The Lewis and Clark Trail.* Harrisburg: Stackpole Books, 1978.

Steffen, Jerome O. *William Clark: Jeffersonian Man on the Frontier.* Norman: University of Oklahoma Press, 1977.

FURTHER READING

Blumberg, Rhoda. *The Incredible Journey of Lewis and Clark.* New York: Lothrop, Lee and Shepard, 1987.

Brown, Marion Marsh. *Sacagawea: Indian Interpreter to Lewis and Clark.* Emeryville, California: Children's Book Press, 1988.

Cavan, Seamus. *Lewis and Clark and the Route to the Pacific.* New York: Chelsea House, 1991.

Kroll, Steven. *Lewis and Clark: Explorers of the American West.* New York: Holiday House, 1994.

Morley, Jacqueline. *Across America: The Story of Lewis and Clark.* New York: Watts, 1998.

Moulton, Gary E. *Lewis and Clark and the Route to the Pacific.* New York: Chelsea House, 1991.

Stefoff, Rebecca. *Lewis and Clark.* New York: Chelsea House, 1992.

FOR MORE INFORMATION

Lewis and Clark National Historic Trail
Madison, Wisconsin
Publishes and distributes a general information brochure and map of the trail. Write for copies.
(700 Rayovac Drive, Suite 100, Madison, WI 53711)

The Lewis and Clark Trail Heritage Foundation
Great Falls, Montana
Write for information about the history of the expedition, publications, local chapter activities, and volunteer projects.
(P.O. Box 3434, Great Falls, MT 59403)

National Lewis and Clark Bicentennial Council
Seattle, Washington
Write for information about the activities that federal, state, and tribal governments are planning for the years 2004 through 2006 to celebrate the bicentennial of the expedition.
(P.O. Box 9559, Seattle, WA 98109-0550)

PHOTO CREDITS

INDEX

Bold numbers refer to photographs